ANOTHER
1001
ONE-LINERS
AND SHORT JOKES

ANOTHER 1001 ONE-LINERS AND SHORT JOKES:

THE ULTIMATE COLLECTION OF THE FUNNIEST, LAUGH-OUT-LOUD, RIB-TICKLERS

GRAHAM CANN

"There is nothing in the world so irresistibly contagious as laughter and good humour"

CHARLES DICKENS

CONTENTS

CLAIM YOUR FREE GIVEAWAY HERE!

When I compiled the trilogy of joke books, **'1001 One-Liners and Short Jokes'**, **'Another 1001 One-Liners and Short Jokes'** and **'1001 Dad Jokes'**, I had so much fun compiling them that I went a bit overboard and ended up with far more jokes than I needed for the three books!

What was I to do with those surplus one-liners?

No contest! I decided to put together all those extra chuckles and titters into a **FREE GIFT just for you, '201 One-Liners and Short Jokes'**. All you have to do to receive this gag-tastic e-book is to use this link **https://dl.bookfunnel.com/n90r726oa8** and I'll send you a copy free, gratis and on the house!

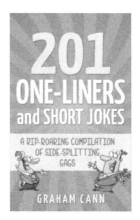

Not only will you receive a free joke book but I'll also enrol you as a member of **The 1001 One-Liners Club** where I send you a light-hearted email every Monday morning to get your week off to a flying start!

THE CURTAIN-RAISER

Welcome along to the second outing of '1001 One-Liners and Short Jokes'. Due to the huge popularity of the first volume, I couldn't resist putting together another massive funny feast for all you good people out there who like nothing better than to revel in inordinate amounts of silliness.

It's been said that 'A pun is not completely matured until it is full groan' and you'll find many ripe fruits waiting to be plucked in this batty batch. There are still a large number of categories that the jokes are filed under and some new ones for good measure.

So go on, grab these jokes and use them to impress your friends or just relax and indulge in a feast of flapdoodle.

Enjoy ☺

Graham Cann

ADDICTIONS

My wife left me because I was a compulsive gambler. I'll do anything to win her back.

I joined a self-help group for people who talk too much called 'On and On Anon'.

I recently returned to speak at the annual Plastic Surgery Addiction Conference. It was great to see some old friends and lots of new faces.

I suffer from CDO. It's like OCD but in alphabetical order.

I got confused with Alcoholics Anonymous and the Automobile Association when I tried to join recently. Either way, I'm on the road to recovery.

I wanted to join Paranoids Anonymous but they wouldn't tell me where they met.

I think that people who collect magazines have got issues.

I went to a water park, tried a couple of slides and now I'm worried I'm getting addicted. It's a slippery slope.

I've just joined a dating site for arsonists. Still waiting for a match.

I tried to talk to my wife about my obsession with balloons. She said I was blowing it up out of all proportion. I feel really let down.

If alcohol can damage your short-term memory, just think what alcohol can do.

If you're addicted to seaweed, sea kelp.

Our whole family is really worried about my grandfather's Viagra addiction. Grandma is taking it particularly hard.

There's the drug addict fisherman who accidentally caught a duck. Now he's hooked on quack.

I'm really obsessed with the F1 key on my keyboard. I'm trying to get help.

My wife left me because of my obsession with pasta. I'm feeling cannelloni right now.

Get stoned. Drink wet cement.

My girlfriend is fed up with my constant wordplay jokes so I asked her 'How can I stop my addiction?' She said 'Whatever means necessary'. I said 'No, it doesn't'.

I can't stop eating Polos, Extra Strong Mints and Tic Tacs. I'm worried I'm going to end up in a menthol institution.

My wife left me because of my obsession with sauces. Oh well, tartar.

I've just caught my kleptomaniac friend stealing my Disney toy. I've put up with a lot from him but this was just taking the Mickey.

I was once a habitual bottom flasher but that was many moons ago.

I've finally been cured of my compulsive buying of boats. Those antibuyyachtics certainly did the trick.

ARTS AND CRAFTS

If Shakespeare had written a work on puns, would that have been a play on words?

A third off books today at Waterstones. I got 'The Lion, The Witch'.

Anyone interested in pressing wild flowers should take a leaf out of my book.

I don't mean to brag but I'm the first person to make a book from onion skins. Read it and weep.

Just finished a great book "The History of Cannibalism" by Henrietta Mann.

I asked the librarian if they had any books on pantomimes. She said 'They're behind you'.

Never ever lose an audio book. You'll never hear the end of it.

I used to have a fear of painting. But I brushed it off.

I bought this book "100 Things To Do Before You Die". I got to 99 and thought I'd better stop reading now.

BREAKING NEWS: Humpty Dumpty was pushed.

Just finished reading 'The History of Soup' – the condensed version.

Dad: 'What's a lion and a witch doing in your wardrobe?'
Son: 'It's Narnia business'.

I was going to be an amateur poet but thought I'd leave it to the prose.

Why did Piglet go to the toilet? To search for Pooh.

I've just written my new book 'The A to C of Laziness'.

My sister asked me to bring her something hard to write on. I don't know why she became so mad. It's pretty bloody hard to write on sand.

I plan on reading a book about torches. Some light reading before bed.

Winnie the Pooh and Christopher Robin really missed Piglet. But they did so enjoy that bacon sandwich.

I can thoroughly recommend the book 'Fights on a Narrowboat' by R. G. Bargee.

The book on chronology that I ordered has finally arrived. It's about time.....

I'm writing a book about hurricanes and tornadoes. It's only a draft at the moment....

I have a book coming out soon. I don't know what possessed me to eat it in the first place.

I was asked yesterday if I'd like some books on 80's hairstyles. I said I'd mullet over.

Someone stole my comics. Marvelless!

I've just finished reading the fifth book in the Learning to Count trilogy.

I've got this pencil that used to be owned by Shakespeare but he chewed the end of it. I can't tell if it's 2B or not 2B.

Although I'm helping a witch to write her biography, I'm doing the spell checking.

Graham Cann

CELEBRITIES

No matter how enraged Germaine Greer is about something, she'll never be more irate than her sister Anne.

Tried an Adam Ant ice cream yesterday. It was nothing special, just a standard vanilla.

I bought a second-hand wardrobe from Bonnie Tyler and every now and then it falls apart.

Sean Connery was asked to leave the animal sanctuary when he stated that he wanted to shave the animals.

I don't agree with these celebrities giving their kids stupid names. Found out today Shania Twain has called her son Choo Choo.

Today I met Bruce Lee's vegetarian brother, Brocco.

Sherlock has died and Dr Watson hasn't paid his rent. He's Holmeless.

Cinderella was annoyed when her photos hadn't arrived. She said 'Someday my prints will come'.

I told my girlfriend I had a crush on Beyonce. She said 'Whatever floats your boat'. I said 'No, that Buoyancy'.

Barack Obama goes to a fancy dress party while giving his wife a piggyback ride. Someone asks him what he's dressed up as and he says 'I'm a snail. And that's M'Shell on my back'.

I'd like to congratulate Michael Caine on the excellent restroom facilities at his new animal park. There were zoo loos. Thousands of them.

Last night I went to see Walt Disney On Ice but it was a huge disappointment. Just an old bloke in a freezer.

Charlie Brown is quitting his job as a cartoon character. He's fed up working for Peanuts.

Someone asked me what Baden-Powell was connected with. I said 'A hyphen'.

How do you find actor Will Smith in a snow drift? Look for the Fresh Prints.

I used to wonder if Elton John liked lettuce but then realised he's more of a rocket man.

Graham Cann

CHILDREN

Daddy, daddy what does transgender mean? I don't know son! Ask your Auntie Herbert.

When I was a baby my parents used to bath me in cheap Australian lager. It wasn't until I was 18 that I realised I'd been fostered.

My friend's four year old child has been learning Spanish all year and still can't say the word 'please' which I think is poor for four.

I've discovered the cheapest place to get kids' shoes is at the front of a bouncy castle.

My wife's carrying our first child. He's eight, the lazy little......

We've had to get a live-in nanny because the dead one wasn't working out.

There was big kidnapping at my son's school today. No panic! He woke up.

We were so poor when I was a child that, when it got cold, we had to sit around a candle. When it got really cold, we used to light it.

When I was a child I wanted to be Aluminium Man so I could foil crime.

My three-year-old son got into the bath with me last night. 'Why is your willy much longer and fatter than mine?' 'I don't know daddy' he replied.

I was so ugly as a baby, when I was born the midwife slapped my mother.

I couldn't afford to take the kids to the Sea Life Centre so we went to the fish market instead. I said 'Sshhh! They're all sleeping'.

Why is it that when someone takes their baby into a baby changing room, they always come out with the same one?

I've got a kid in Africa that I feed, that I clothe, that I school, that I inoculate for 75 cents a day. Which is practically nothing compared to what it cost to send him there.

It turns out that when you're asked to pick your favourite child, you're supposed to pick one of your own. I know that now.

I said to my wife 'I saw a woman with her breasts out on the bus feeding her son'. She said 'It's natural'. 'Natural?' I replied. 'She was feeding him crisps'.

To the person who stole my shoes while I was on the bouncy castle. How childish!

The lad who sat next to me at school one day ate his calculator. Everybody said he was a weirdo but like I said 'It's what's inside him that counts'.

My nickname at school was Scarface. I was brilliant at knitting.

CHRISTMAS

I always carry a pebble in my pocket in October to throw at people singing Christmas songs. I call it my jingle bell rock.

We should ban Carol singing. I've heard her and she's awful.

I hear they're banning glitter this Christmas. Well, it's been on the cards for years.

An affluent Christmas is a rich yule in our house.

The kids want a dog for Christmas. I was going to do turkey as normal.....

If anyone is alone with no-one to spend Christmas with, please let me know. I need to borrow some chairs.

My parents really treated me badly when I was a kid. One year I opened my Christmas present and it was just an empty box. They told me it was an Action Man deserter.

My job reminds me of Christmas every day. I do all the hard work and some fat bloke in a suit takes all the credit.

What nationality is Santa Claus? North Polish.

Santa's elves are just a bunch of subordinate Clauses.

What do you get when you cross a snowman with a vampire? Frostbite.

I was wondering if anyone can remember the day when your parents told you that Santa didn't exist. When they told me, I was so upset, I jumped in my car and headed to the pub......

WARNING: If you get a link called 'Ronan Keating sings Christmas carols' don't open it! It's a link to Ronan Keating singing Christmas carols.

I like to decorate the Christmas tree with the kids but they're getting older. It's harder to find branches that support their weight.

We're having octopus for Christmas dinner this year. Tastes awful but everyone gets a leg.

The days of advent calendars are numbered.

I've decided to release a Christmas record 'Duvet know it's Christmas'. It's a cover version.

Graham Cann

CREATURES

What do I know about Shetland ponies? Very little.

You can always tell the gender of ants just by placing them in water. If they sink, girl ant. If they float, buoyant.

A bloke takes two monkeys to a taxidermist. 'Would you like them mounted, sir?' 'I'd be happy with them just shaking hands thanks.'

I just killed a huge spider running across the floor with my shoe. I don't care how big the spider is, no-one steals my shoe.

I took my crocodile away on a weekend break. I got some great snaps.

Two parrots were sitting on a perch. One said to the other 'Can you smell fish?'

Two silk worms had a race. They both ended up in a tie.

'OMG there's a wolf'. 'Where?' 'No, the normal kind'.

A penguin goes into a pub and says to the barman 'Has my brother been in?' Barman: 'What does he look like?'

I recently bought a pair of snail skin shoes. It took me seven hours to walk out the shop.There's been a spike in the sighting of hedgehogs.

What goes peck, peck, bang? A chicken in a minefield.

What do zebras have that no other animal has? Baby zebras.

The amazing fact about ants is that they never get sick. They have anty bodies.

I can get quite nervous when I raise caterpillars as pets. It always gives me butterflies.

The least interesting beast in the animal kingdom has to be a boar.

Why do cows have hooves? Because they lactose.

I was walking in the jungle and I saw this lizard on his hind legs telling some brilliant jokes. I turned to a local tribesman and said 'That lizard's really funny'. He said 'That's not a lizard. He's a stand-up chameleon'.

There's a species of kangaroo that can jump higher than the average house. This is due to its powerful legs and the fact that the average house cannot jump.

My cow has just wandered into a field of marijuana. The steaks have never been so high...........

Whether Dumbo could fly or not is totally irrelephant.

A cow escaped her field by jumping over a low barbed wire fence. Udder destruction.

My 30' snake died today. So long.

I'm not being paranoid but there's a dozen Peruvian owls perched on my fence staring through the window. I think they must be Inca hoots.

The staff at London Zoo didn't seem to appreciate my Rod Hull impression. To be fair, neither did the emu.

What's the fastest way to massacre snails? A salt rifle.

An anteater walks into a bar.
Bartender: 'Can I get you a drink?'
Anteater: 'Noooooooooooooooooooo'.
Bartender: 'Well, how about a gin and tonic?'
Anteater: 'Noooooooooooooooooo'.
Bartender: 'What's with the big no's?'

I read the other day that humans eat more bananas than monkeys. It comes as no surprise to me as everyone I know has never eaten a monkey.

Once when I was staying at a Moscow hotel, I was stung by a dodgy looking wasp. Although now I suspect it was the cagey bee.

Skunks celebrate St Valentine's Day because they're so scent-imental.

Hitting birds is illegal and if you do, you get a big fine. I learnt this when I kicked a pelican. I ended up footing a massive bill.

A bee that lives in America is known as a USB.

What do you call a frog stuck in mud? Unhoppy.

What do crabs smoke? Seaweed.

I went on an illegal grouse hunt the other day but once they started flying I knew the game was up.

What do you call an explosive monkey? A baboom.

Before the crowbar was invented, most crows drank at home.

I've just been thrown out of my local park after arranging the squirrels by height. They didn't like me critter sizing.

I can describe a hungry horse in four letters. MTGG.

I've combined a degree in taxidermy with my bomb making skills and come up with an otter you can't defuse.

For my friend on his birthday, I bought him an elephant for his room. He said 'Thanks very much'. I said 'Don't mention it'.

I got thrown out of Chester Zoo yesterday for making a parrot laugh. It's polly tickle correctness gone mad.

I've just been attacked by a herd of hungry cows. I'm OK but I've been badly grazed.

Won my first cage fight last night. The budgie stood no chance.

Goats mate for life. They stay together for the sake of the kids.

I saw two naked snails having a fight last night. I was going to break it up but decided to let them slug it out.

Where do crabs in London get a train to go on their holidays? Kings Crustacean.

I was successful in my interview and trial for this job of packing tiny insects into containers to be sent off for medical research. I boxed all the ticks.

I'm thinking of buying a greyhound but not sure what the missus will say. I'd better run it by her first.

I spotted a lizard on a portable toilet. It was one of those commode-o-dragons.

DEATH

On my tombstone I want it to say: 'Failed to forward chain letter to five friends'.

The woman next door to me is a golf widow. Her husband got run over by a Volkswagen.

A man tried to sell me a coffin yesterday. I told him 'That's the last thing I need'.

Wife: 'He died of natural causes'.
Detective: 'You pushed him off the roof'.
Wife: 'Gravity is natural'.

On my gravestone I want the wording 'Here lies Graham, who was always thinking outside the box. Not now obviously'.

The eyes are one of the last parts of your body to die. They dilate.

What's the difference between a Lamborghini and a pile of dead bodies? I don't have a Lamborghini in my garage.

I hate how funerals are always at 9am. I'm not really a mourning person.

Don't challenge the Grim Reaper to a pillow fight. Unless you're prepared for the Reaper cushions.

One of my friends was killed when a coffee machine fell on top of him. Thankfully, it was instant.

How did the reporter kill himself? Noosepaper.

When people ask how my grandfather died, I always say that it was drink that killed him. He was run over by a Guinness truck.

When I die, I want something special. I want to be chopped up into 195 parts and a piece of me left in every country in the world. That's me all over.

I got the sack from the Samaritans. I got a call from a man saying he was going to kill himself by standing in front of a train. I told him to stay on the line.

A funeral was held today for the inventor of air conditioning. Thousands of fans attended.

Graham Cann

DENTISTS

What do you call a dentist who doesn't like tea? Denis.

My usual dentist is away so I had a temporary filling in.

Graham Cann

DOCTORS

What did the doctor tell the man who'd swallowed a golf ball? It's gone down a fair way.

My doctor asked if I had trouble passing water. I said that I usually get the shakes passing the duck pond.

Doctor: 'Your body has run out of magnesium'. Patient: 'Omg'

A man recently had a severely negative reaction after licking a postage stamp. Doctors decided it was anaphilatelic shock.

I was sorry to hear recently of the plastic surgeon who sat by his fire and melted.

I had to tell my patient that I'd completely botched up his plastic surgery operation. I'll never forget the look on his elbow.

Me: 'Doctor, I had a nasty reaction when I applied cream to my piles'.
Doctor: 'Where did you apply it?'
Me: 'On the bus'.

My doctor asked me if I wanted the good news or the bad news. I said 'Good news'. He said 'Well, we're naming the disease after you'.

Receptionist: 'I've scheduled your appointment for 4:45pm as the doctor said you were the last person he wanted to see'.

I told my doctor that every time I pass through one country to another I need a drink. He told me I'm borderline alcoholic.

I rang the receptionist at my doctor's and said I needed an appointment. 'OK' she said 'How about 10 tomorrow?' I said 'No I don't need that many'.

I went to the doctors today and told him I can't stop thieving. He said 'That's not good. Take these tablets for two weeks and if they don't work, get me a 50" Plasma TV'.

Doctor: 'I've got some bad news and some really bad news'.
Patient: 'What's the bad news?'
Doctor: 'You've got two days to live'.
Patient: 'What's the really bad news?'
Doctor: 'I should have told you yesterday'.

A pirate went to the doctor and said 'I have moles on me back'. The doctor said 'It's OK, they're benign'. The pirate replied 'Count again, I think there be ten'.

Doctors are saying not to worry about bird flu. It's tweetable.

Doctor: 'Sir, I'm afraid your DNA is backwards'.
Patient: 'And?'

A doctor is always calm because he has lots of patients.

I once woke up in the middle of an operation. 'Doctor, thank goodness you're awake! Your patient's dying!' said my fellow surgeons. I never practised as an anaesthetist ever again.

A man called 999. 'My friend and I were walking through the woods when he collapsed. I think he's died'. 'OK' said the operator. 'First, make sure he's dead'. There's a silence followed by a gunshot. Then the man got back on the line. 'And now what?'

There was only one way to cure the Invisible Man. Doctors took him to the ICU.

My doctor has asked me for a stool sample so I've enrolled on a 3 week basic wood turning course.

Patient: 'Is it serious, doc?'
Doctor: 'If I were you, I wouldn't buy any green bananas'.

Patient: 'Doctor, I think my brother's going crazy'.
Doctor: 'Why?'
Patient: 'He thinks he's a chicken'.
Doctor: 'Well, why don't you have him committed?'
Patient: 'I would have but we need the eggs'.

My hospital doctor friend has a picture of a country estate next to his bed. It's noticeable that he has a good bedside manor.

I mistakenly ate daffodil bulbs instead of garlic and I'm now in hospital. Anyway, I should be out in the spring.

So I said to my doctor 'I've got an ingrowing toenail, athlete's foot and sweaty feet'. He said 'I wouldn't like to be in your shoes'.

Patient: 'I keep thinking I'm Mickey Mouse one minute and Pluto the next.
Doctor: 'How long have you been having these Disney spells?'

I accidentally drank a bottle of invisible ink last night. I'm now in hospital waiting to be seen.

I parked up in the hospital car park and this official bloke said that the space I was in was reserved for badge holders only. I said I had a bad shoulder.

I get a sore shoulder when I bowl googlies. I need a spin doctor.

Patient: 'Will I be able to play the violin after the operation?'
Doctor: 'Of course you will'.
Patient: 'That's great! I couldn't play one before'.

Doctor: 'You've only got 10 to live'.
Patient: '10 what? Years months, weeks...?'
Doctor: '9'.

A chap goes to see the doctor with salt in one ear and pepper in the other. The doctor said 'You need to start eating more sensibly'.

Two months after my operation, the doctor says I can start to do some light housework. The trouble is I live 70 miles from the coast.

Graham Cann

DO IT YOURSELF

I've read Plumbing for Idiots twice and I still haven't got a clue what I'm doing. I guess it's going to take another few reads before this sinks in.

The results from my home DNA test have come back and apparently I'm 50% vampire. I'm so ashamed I can't even look at myself in the mirror.

Is there anyone called Philip out there? I found your screwdriver.

I can count the number of chainsaw accidents I've had on the fingers of one hand.

I went to a fancy dress party last night dressed as a harp. The host told me I was too small to be dressed as a harp. I said 'Are you calling me a lyre?'

My wife wondered I was wearing two jackets when I painted our house. I said 'The instructions on the can clearly state – put on two coats'.

Just finished the deepest well in England when I realised I had the plans round the wrong way. Started work on the tallest lighthouse....

I'm feeling very proud of myself today. I fitted a Bannister in under four minutes.

I remember the first day learning to build a wall. I was bricking it.

I couldn't get a good picture on the TV so the wife said 'Try the aerial on the roof'. Now I still haven't got a good picture and I've got piles of washing powder all over the tiles.

My plans to build a bungalow had one flaw.

ENTERTAINMENT

Just watched the final of the lumberjack World Championships on TV. Tree fellers from Ireland won it.

I'm heading down to the Autopsy Club later. It's an open Mike night...............

I've been really trying to get my young horse into the Magic Circle but despite all my efforts, he's still only a one trick pony.

I got kicked out of the cinema last night for bringing my own food in with me. I was gutted. It's ages since I've had a barbecue.

In his early years Houdini used a trapdoor in his act. It was just a stage he was going through.

I've bought a skeleton costume for a Halloween party but I've got nobody to go with.

I was disappointed when I saw The Mousetrap at the theatre. It looked nothing like the board game I had as a kid.

Just watched a documentary about Albert Einstein. Apparently he was a very nice man unlike his brother Frank.

I knew it was Michael J Fox I saw in the garden centre. He had his back to the fuchsias.

I've just seen a TV documentary about beavers. It was the best dam programme I've ever seen.

People ask me how I smuggle chocolate into the cinema. Well, I have a few Twix up my sleeve.

I've just sold my entire collection of Sooty, Sweep and Sue puppets. Someone is paying me £200 to take them off my hands.

Not many people know that Yoda had a last name. It was Layheehoo.

I can't wait for the RNLI annual party. They really know how to push the boat out.

The entrance fee to our local aquarium has been waived as long as you are either camping or dressed as a dolphin. To all intents and porpoises, it's free.

It's sad how Wile E. Coyote is remembered for his violence and not for his brilliantly realistic paintings of tunnels.

When they asked for volunteer ventriloquists, I was the first to put my hand up.

My late grandmother was such a fan of Thunderbirds puppets. When she got seriously ill, she insisted we kept a Virgil at her bedside.

There's a new channel for origami enthusiasts. However, it's paper view.

I got a part in the movie 'Cocaine'. I only have one line.

I tried watching The Neverending Story but I just couldn't finish it.

What do you call a dead magician? An abra-cadaver.

They're doing a sequel to 'Finding Dory' where she discovers she has cancer and searches for a cure. It's called Finding Chemo.

I've got a small acting part in a television commercial for a well-known soap. It's only a Camay-o appearance.

It's so hard to find Gandalf impersonators. You can't get the staff.

I used to be a pantomime horse but I quit while I was a head.

What do you call Batman after he gets beaten up? Bruised Wayne.

What do you call a magician without magic? Ian.

We produced a play about the weather and needed eight children to be clouds. We ended up having twelve so we were a bit overcast.

I've just been expelled from my mime class. Must have been something I said.

Lord of the Rings? Now you're Tolkien.

Anyone interested in my Bugs Bunny videos? I'm getting a bit long in the tooth for them.

So I said to the Daleks: 'Why don't you just have an apple a day?'

The Honourable Society of Ventriloquists is holding its Annual Fete tomorrow and it includes a gouncy castle, gottled geer, hangurgers and lots nore.

EVERYDAY OBJECTS

I can't understand why my calculator has stopped working. It just doesn't add up.

Why are my clothes so creased? It must be an iron deficiency.

I have a pen that actually writes underwater. It can write other words too.

Somebody stole my Army colouring book. I'm looking for a soldier to crayon.

I wonder what went off in Thomas Edison's head before he invented the light bulb......

I've just bumped into the man who invented the globe. It's a small world.

A bloke in the pub said to me 'Are those thick Lens glasses you're wearing?' I said 'No, they're mine'.

These toilet brushes are awful. I had one for a while but I gave up on it and went back to using paper.

I feel so strongly about graffiti in toilet cubicles, I've signed a partition.

My house is so cold that when I open the door, the light comes on.

I got rid of the clothes horse I've had for 25 years. It was the end of an airer.

Two windmills standing in a field. One asks the other 'What music do you like?' The other says 'I'm a big metal fan'.

When the chair was invented, the inventor's friend wanted to know what it did. The inventor replied 'You might want to sit down for this'.

A fire hydrant has H-2-0 on the inside and K-9-P on the outside.

I've just bought a TV and it says 'Built in Antenna'. I don't even know where that is.

Finding a woman sobbing because she'd locked her car keys in her car, a passing soldier, assessing the situation, removed his trousers and rubbed them against the car door which magically opened. 'That's so clever', gasped the woman. 'How did you do it?' 'Easy', said the soldier. 'These are my khakis'.

If there were an award for the least effective way to clean things, I would sweep the table.

My mobile hair dresser is coming round today. About time too! I'm fed up with my hairy phone.

Making your water bed more bouncy requires spring water.

Me and the wife tried sprucing up our marriage after 40 years so we bought a water bed. Things were great for a few weeks but then I felt us drifting apart.

How much does a Cockney spend on shampoo? Pantene.

FAMILIES

My wife was upset and said I never treat her any more. I said to myself that she was right so I went to town and bought her a bag and a belt. I tell you what, the Hoover runs like a dream now.

After watching a TV programme about the phenomenon of mixed emotions I said to my wife 'I bet you can't tell me anything that will make me happy and sad at the same time'. She said 'Out of all your friends, you've got the biggest penis'.

My wife said I have two major faults. I don't listen ....and something else.

My grandad died falling through a deckchair. RIP.

My dad used to say when one door closes another one opens. He was a terrible cabinet maker.

My wife just opened the door for me. Would have been a nice gesture had we not been going 70mph.

My grandma is 96 years old and still doesn't need glasses. She drinks straight from the bottle.

My grandfather had his tongue shot off while serving in France during the last war. He never talked about it.

When I was making a cup of tea for me and the wife I shouted to her 'Do you want a Kit Kat Chunky?' I don't remember much after that.

For my wife's birthday, I bought her 5 litres of Castrol commercial truck lubricant for £35. When she asked me what it was I said 'Lorry Oil. Because you're worth it.'

Amal and Juan are identical twins. Their mum only carries one photo because once you've seen Juan you've seen Amal.

My wife glared at me this morning. 'Did you eat that chocolate in the fridge last night?' I said 'No, I ate it on the sofa.'

My brother threw another piece of cheese at me, although that was mild compared to the previous night. How immature! How dairy?

My wife complains I never buy her jewellery. In my defence, I never knew she sold jewellery.

I went past the house where I grew up the other day. I knocked and asked if I could have a look around and they slammed the door in my face. My parents can be really obnoxious at times.

My aunt and uncle have made a fortune selling lamb chops. They're minted.

My wife has just announced she's leaving me because of my obsession with American sitcoms. Happy Days!

I can't believe it, my son came home today with two armchairs and a sofa. I've told him a million times not to accept suites from strangers.

My wife just said she can't take any more of my laziness. As soon as my mum comes round to pack my bags, I'm leaving.

The wife and I have been going to marriage guidance.
Wife: 'He misunderstands everything!'
Counsellor (to me): 'What does she mean?'
Me: 'It's a feminine pronoun'.
It's not going well.......

My husband's been hanging out at the gym. I told him he should wear bigger shorts.

My grandad spent his whole life in the kebab business and hoped I'd follow in his footsteps but I didn't. He was buried with all his equipment and now he's probably turning in his grave.

I found a present for my mother-in-law in the loft. I'll take it up to her later.

My wife is blaming me for ruining her birthday. That's ridiculous! I didn't even know it was her birthday.

My grandfather was a baker in the Army. When he went to war, he went in with all buns glazing.

My wife asked me if I could clear the table. I had to get a running start but I made it!

I remember the last thing my nan said to me before she died. 'What are you doing with that hammer?'

My wife has locked herself in the kitchen in a rage after a massive argument over how tight I've become since we've been married. She's in there now ripping all the plates in half.

I tried to re-marry my ex-wife but she figured out I was only after my money.

What do you say to your sister when she's upset? 'Are you having a crisis?'

My husband said to me 'There's a man knocking at the door with a beard'. I said 'No wonder I didn't hear him'.

My wife threatened to divorce me if I gave our daughter a silly name. So I called her Bluff.

Having a teenage daughter is like having a cat that only comes out to eat and hisses when you try to be nice.

My husband has told me he's given up smoking. To see if he's telling the truth, I've left the gas on and gone to work.

A father started washing his car with his 5 year-old son. After a while, the son said 'Do you think you could use a sponge instead?'

My sister is the world's worst cook. She tried combining corned beef, potato and onion - made a right hash of it.

Today my son asked 'Can you lend me a book mark?' I immediately burst into tears. 12 years old and he doesn't know my name's Brian.

My father worked 12 hours a day to put food on the table. Great dad, slow cook.

Which part of your family can you see through? A transparent.

I lost my daughter's cosmetic bag. I wonder how I'll make up for this mistake.

It's normal for married couples to fight. The trick is for you and your spouse to find a couple you can easily beat up.

'Dad, can you tell me what a solar eclipse is like?'
'No sun'.

My dad taught me to swim by throwing me into the river. It was easy once I'd got out of the sack.

My grandad was a one liner comedian. His only gig was on the Titanic.

I caught my daughter chewing on a power cable so I had to ground her.

Last year I wanted to buy a present for my niece so I asked her parents what she was in to presently. They replied 'Anything Frozen'. So I bought her oven chips and a bag of peas.

My wife said she was OK about me having a tattoo. Now she's moaning about the bagpipers in the back garden.

My auntie was a lollipop lady. She had a very thin body and a big sticky head.

My brother accidentally swallowed some weed killer. Fortunately, he saw the fungicide.

I'm Caucasian. My mum's from a city in Ireland and my dad's Japanese.

Graham Cann

FOOD AND DRINK

I opened a tin of evaporated milk. It was empty.

People who say onions make you cry have obviously never been hit in the face with a turnip.

I've been desperately trying to lose some weight lately but I've just had too much on my plate.

I worry about cured ham. What was wrong with it in the first place?

I went to an Indian restaurant last night. After I ordered, a little old lady came to me and said 'Aren't you polite. You have such lovely manners.' Apparently, it was my complimentary nan.

There's just been an explosion in a French cheese factory. Da brie is everywhere.

The next person that asks for pineapple juice, cranberry juice, lemonade and a slice of orange in the same glass is gonna get a punch.

I used to wonder why people paid a fortune for those little bottles of Evian water until I read it backwards……

I went in a fish and chip shop and asked for a large plaice. He said 'It won't be long'. I said 'It better be wide then'.

I wasn't the only one involved in the sandwich shop robbery but it was me who took the wrap.

I don't wish to brag but I just ate my lunch without taking a picture of it first.

Sad news about the French chef who topped himself. He lost the huile d'olive.

What scary cake keeps coming back? A boo meringue.

I used to be indecisive about chicken casseroles but now I'm not chasseur.

The patron saint of checking if your bread rolls are ready to come out of the oven is St John the Bap Test.

Not enough people are eating salads. I think that needs addressing.

When I eat bacon, I lose my memory. I've been told it's Hamnesia.

Mum was cooking in the kitchen. I yelled out 'Mummy can I lick the bowl?' She said 'No, you can flush just like everyone else'.

The chef in our local restaurant has been made redundant. I've asked him to let me know how things pan out.

Chocolate is not in my vocadbury.

I've started rubbing ketchup in my eyes every morning. Everyone says things are so much better with Heinzsight.

The French enjoy eating snails because they don't like fast food.

My Scottish mate is very worried about being arrested for illegally making porridge in his wellies. He's quaking in his boots.

Tesco have announced that they will be adding a new beer to their value range of real ales. Alongside the affordable Simply Golden Ale and the inexpensive Simply Dark, they're adding Simply Red for when money's too tight to mention.

I had a glass of the best milk I've ever tasted today. It was legend dairy.

We had a bite to eat in our local village – Horse and Hounds. I won't be ordering that again.

I thought coq au vin was love in a lorry.

I've been telling people about the benefit of eating dried grapes. It's all about raisin awareness.

I went to my local curry house and ordered the special which was pelican curry. It was delicious but the bill was huge.

What do you call a fake noodle? An impasta.

Have you ever tried Chinese dumplings? They really are the dogs bollocks.

I just learned that French fries are not from France at all. They were first cooked in Greece.

How do you introduce a hamburger? Meat pattie.

Tea bags are going up in price. Anger is brewing across the nation.

My liquid diet is going really well. After six glasses of wine, I don't care how fat I am.

I've got a joke about a fish but this isn't the thyme or plaice for it.

I just phoned my local restaurant and asked if they do takeaways and they said 'Yes'. So I said 'What's 157 minus 73?'

I stopped by a roadside stand selling lobster tails for $2. I paid my $2 and he said 'Once upon a time there was this lobster.....'

I like to use German wine in my cooking on an add hoc basis.

Reports are coming in of a huge explosion in a baking powder factory. Police are expecting casualties to rise.

The Greek cheese industry is secretly controlled by the Hallouminati.

How do you make any salad into a Caesar salad? Stab it twenty- three times.

I ate a Kid's Meal at Macdonalds today. His mum was furious.

Cadbury's have just delivered a giant chocolate bar to The Bank of England. It's a massive Boost for the economy.

Our dog is now completely bald and I feel sicker than ever. Can anyone suggest a different hangover remedy?

I was sitting drinking coffee in my slippers this morning when I thought to myself 'I really need to wash some mugs'.

I tried to join Weight Watchers last night. I went to create an account online only to be asked 'Do you accept cookies?' I think it's a test.

I'm just finishing my sandwich filling degree. I do my final eggs ham tomorrow....

I've just seen on the news that there is a dangerous Welsh cheese on the loose. Police say that if you see this cheese, then please approach it Caerphilly.

I relish the fact that you've mustard the strength to ketchup to me.

A vegan said to me 'People who sell meat are gross!' I said 'People who sell fruit and vegetables are grocer'.

The recipe said 'Set the oven to 180 degrees' so I did. But now I can't open the door because it's facing the wall.

What's the most dangerous thing in your fridge? Ice is.

What do tofu and a dildo have in common? They're both meat substitutes.

Pork and leek – great name for sausages. Lousy brand name for condoms.

The cheapest meat you can buy right now are deer balls. They're under a buck.

Somebody just threw a jar of mayonnaise at me. I was like 'What the Hellman?'

Drinking tea while being too relaxed can kill you. It's called a casual tea.

Greggs have just announced plans to start a home delivery service using drones. All sounds a bit pie in the sky to me........

Cadbury's have denied rumours that they're phasing out one of their popular chocolate bars. It's flake news.

You can't put too many mushrooms on a pizza. Because you won't have much room for anything else.

There have been arguments between tea growing companies. Trouble is brewing and relationships are strained.

I've just tried magic mushrooms. Great result – 5 stars on Trip Advisor.

Sad to hear they're not making shortbread any longer.

Very sad news. My relationship with whisky is on the rocks.

So I got this box of Celebrations and swapped all the wrappers around. When my wife had one, she got her Snickers in a Twix.

For every rich tea biscuit, there are a hundred ordinary tea biscuits living in poverty.

'Muffins' spelt backwards is what you do when you take them out of the oven.

I'm delighted to announce that I'm opening a new seafood restaurant. All are whelk come.

I broke a tooth eating a cottage pie. I'd forgotten to remove the bricks.

Is it OK to dip bread in a curry? Asking for my naan.

I took my girlfriend to a fancy restaurant. I had steak, she had frogs legs and chicken breasts but a smashing personality.

Say what you like about waiters but I think they do bring a lot to the table.

Boiled eggs. You can't beat them.

My friend Joe recently went on the Dolly Parton diet. It really made Joe lean, Joe lean, Joe lean, Joe lean.....

I went to a new Indian restaurant called Karma. No menu. You get what you deserve.

A man wearing a tie fastener walks into a bar. The barman says 'We don't like your tie pin here'.

What's yellow, smells of almonds and swings from cake to cake? Tarzipan.

I was in a restaurant the other evening and I ordered a Napoleon chicken for the first time. When it came, there was no meat, just a carcass. I said 'What's this?' She said 'It's the boney part'.

FRIENDS

I went to a friend's party last night and some idiot put a teabag in my mouth. I went mental and totally lost it. No-one treats me like a mug!

My girlfriend's always trying to put me down. One of the disadvantages of going out with a vet.

You offer someone a sincere compliment on their moustache and suddenly she's not your friend any more.

My friend is a hangman and he told me that work is quiet at the moment so he's going to open a drop-in centre.

My ex used to hit me with stringed instruments. If only I'd known about his history of violins.

My girlfriend wants to leave me because of my obsession with police dramas. She said 'I think we should split up'. I said 'Good idea. We can cover more ground that way'.

I didn't know my girlfriend was a ghost until she walked through the door.

My girlfriend's dog died so to cheer her up I got her an identical one. She was livid! 'What am I going to do with two dead dogs?'

Be wary if your girlfriend wants a dominatrix outfit. They're usually white and flowing with a veil.

I'm dating a girl who loves to be covered in cheese. She's a cracker.

My inuit friend emailed me the other day asking why I never answer when he phones. I hate cold callers.

My housemate thinks our house is haunted but I've lived here for 500 years and haven't noticed anything.

To impress my date I told her I raced horses. She suddenly became more interested and asked casually if I'd been successful. I had to tell her I hadn't beaten one yet.....

My girlfriend and I often laugh about how competitive we are. But I laugh more.

Instead of calling the toilet 'the john', my American friend now calls it 'the jim'. That way it sounds better when she says she goes to the jim every morning.

My good friend is a vegan transgender. He was a herbefore.

My friend asked me 'Why are you always walking ahead of me?' I said 'I'm sorry, I don't follow you'.

I once went out with a girl from Merthyr Tydfil. She said 'Do you want to come back to mine?' So I did. It was a long way down.

I met this chap at a party and I said 'Come outside and I'll show you a good time'. So he did and I ran 100 metres in 11.87 seconds.

My girlfriend's such a bad cook she uses the smoke alarm as a timer.

My best mates and I played a game of hide and seek. It went on for hours and hours……good friends are hard to find.

My buddy set me up on a blind date and said 'Heads up, she's expecting a baby'. I felt like an idiot in the bar just wearing a nappy.

Adam's girlfriend, Ruth, fell off the back of his motorcycle. He just rode on.....Ruthless.

I once dated a girl with a lazy eye. It turns out she was seeing someone else on the side.

It's not going well with my anorexic girlfriend. I'm just seeing less and less of her.

My friend keeps saying 'Cheer up man, it could be worse. You could be stuck underground in a hole full of water'. I know he means well.

One minute my girlfriend is asking me to stop cross dressing and when I argue about it, she tells me to put myself in her shoes.

I looked across the museum hall and spotted my ex-girlfriend but I was too self-conscious to say 'Hello'. There was just too much history between us.

My friend used to think he was a chocolate orange. We had to have him sectioned.

I witnessed an argument between an auctioneer and a hairdresser. They were going at it hammer and tongs.

Him: 'And if we have a second date, I'll buy you flowers'.
Her: 'Orchids?'
Him: 'That's jumping the gun a bit'.

My girlfriend says I'm tight so to prove her wrong we went out for some tea and biscuits. It was quite exciting as she's never given blood before.

I'm just waiting for a friend of mine to call round for a cheese party but he's late. When's Lee Dale going to get here?

A mate of mine threw himself from the twelfth floor of a block of flats. He thought it was the thirteenth, but that's another storey.

A friend of mine has gone into business by setting up a garage that fixes car ignitions. It's a start up.

Graham Cann

GARDENING

I tried to make a belt using aromatic plants. It was a complete waist of thyme.

They say you should never go back to a firework once it's been lit. Our back garden's been out of bounds since 1987.

Someone told me to try horse manure on my rhubarb. I have to say I still prefer custard.

GROWING OLD

I remember when I could stand up without sound effects.

As I get older, I reflect on life. I remember the people I've lost. Perhaps a tour guide wasn't my best career choice.

I just realised that I haven't done the hokey cokey in over 20 years. I guess when you get older you just forget what it's all about.

What has 90 balls and screws old ladies? Bingo.

There's been a change of mind by the local council over the naming of the road next to the new housing complex for the elderly. 'St Peter's Close' seemed somewhat inappropriate.

I needed a potty in the bedroom as I have to keep going to the loo during the night so I went to the local chemist's. The assistant said they didn't stock them and that I should try Boots. I said that I already had, but it flooded out of the lace holes.

HEALTH

I ruined my health by drinking to everyone else's.

Pacemakers will always have a place in my heart.

I've just bought a book on medical procedures. I opened it up and the appendix was missing.

When I get a headache, I do what it says on the bottle. I take two aspirin and keep away from children.

The Nobel Prize for Medicine has gone to the notable Russian Benylin Forchestikov and his work in developing a throat syrup.

I can't believe how much my glasses weigh. I got on the scales and I weighed 10 stone. I then put my glasses on and it said 18 stone.

I was told that you could view a solar eclipse through a colander. I tried it and ended up straining my eyes.

I met a girl whose face is allergic to cosmetics. Honestly, you couldn't make it up.

This Monday it's Diarrhoea Awareness week. It runs all week.

I had my leg X-rayed at my local hospital health check today. The doctor said 'Your patella measures 2.54cm'. I said 'Inch-high knees?' He said '你这个笨蛋'.

Towels are the leading cause of dry skin.

Whoever said laughter is the best medicine clearly hasn't tried curing diarrhoea with a tickle fight.

If you're going to tell jokes about eyes, then the cornea the better.

You know that when you visit the Urologist's department urine good hands.

I used to have an open mind but my brains kept falling out.

My mother-in-law has a massive case of diarrhoea. She won't find out until she gets home and unpacks her luggage.....

They told me I had type A blood but it was a Type O.

I ran into a lamppost yesterday. Luckily, I only sustained light injuries.

A man was rushed into hospital last night with six plastic horses stuck up his arse. The doctors described his condition as stable.

Does anyone remember when I made a joke about chiropractors? It was about a weak back.

I hope the guy who stole my depression tablets is happy now.

Why do opticians have signs above their doors?

I've just heard a friend of mine has sadly contracted leprosy. I think I'll give him a bell.

I've just bought a first aid kid. I thought I'd treat myself.

I bought a home pregnancy kit. Turns out my house is pregnant.

I've just got back from hospital. They reckon I might have pneumonoultramicroscopicsilicovolcanoconiosis. But at the moment, it's hard to say.

Recently I've been getting pins and needles in my leg. My GP couldn't help so I tried alternative medicine. The acupuncturist didn't help much.....

Midwives deserve a lot of respect. They really help people out.

I won't sleep until I find a cure for my insomnia.

Graham Cann

HISTORY

Out of all of King Arthur's knights, I was the most qualified – Sir Tifficate.

So I said to King Canute, that's another pair of shoes ruined.

William the Conqueror won so many battles, I can't help wondering if he cheated by soaking himself in vinegar.

What did Spartacus do to the cannibal who ate his nagging wife? Nothing, he's gladiator.

Why were the Middle Ages called the Dark Ages? There were too many knights.

Where does Napoleon keep his armies? In his sleevies.

A century ago, two brothers insisted that it was possible to fly and as you can see, they were Wright.

It has always been assumed that when a Roman chariot collided with Queen Bodicea's chariot, it was England's first woad accident.

Lance is a relatively uncommon name these days but in medieval times, people were named Lance a lot.

Before she met Henry, Anne had a short-term contract working with skittles. She was Tempin Boleyn.

HOBBIES

Just heard on the news that three Cliff Walkers have fallen to their deaths. I can't believe they had the same name.

I got into a Scrabble throwing fight. It was all fun and games until someone lost an 'i'.

Do gun manuals have a troubleshooting section?

I'm quite interested in learning more about campanology. If you can help, give me a ring.

Four lepers playing cards One of them threw his hand in.

I moved a pawn and it hurt. I moved my knight and I was in agony. Moved my queen and I was doubled up. I think I'm having chess pains.

Feeling chuffed that I've just finished a 30 piece jigsaw in 1 hour. It says on the box 3-5 years........

The inventor of yodelling has recently died. Sadly, so did his little old lady too.

In a freak accident today, a photographer was killed when a huge lump of cheddar landed on him. To be fair, the people who were being photographed did try to warn him.

When I go fishing I play music. I like something catchy.

I put a post on Facebook a few weeks ago saying I was going to climb Mount Everest with no support or equipment. Just to let you all know that I made it up.

I'm not going to bungee jump. I was born because of broken rubber and I'm not going to die the same way.

When was the last time you got a fishing hook stuck in your head? Cast your mind back.

Someone has glued my pack of cards together. I don't know how to deal with it.

I met my wife in a castanets class. We just clicked.

I'm taking part in a stair climbing competition later today. Looking at the other contestants, I need to step up my game.

My Czech mate is surprisingly bad at chess.

When I lost my Playstation 5, there was no consoling me.

I'm sure my wife has been putting glue on my weapons collection. She denies it but I'm sticking to my guns.

I went out for a run yesterday but had to go back soon after because I'd forgotten something. I'd forgotten I was fat, out of shape and couldn't run for more than two minutes.

I don't have the inclination to go hill walking.

Whilst jogging this morning I ran under a ladder, saw a black cat and broke a mirror. A run of bad luck.

For Sale: Limbo dancing equipment. £10. Won't go any lower.

I've been a rodeo rider for two years now, on and off.

I was out fishing yesterday and I couldn't believe it when I reeled in a conger eel. There were twenty other fish hanging on the back of it.

My brother took going to jail really badly. He refused food and drinks, spat and swore at anyone who came near him and started throwing things everywhere. After that, we never played Monopoly again.

My mate used to use liquorice as bait. He caught All Sorts.

I've had to stop Morris dancing. I fell through the windscreen.

I entered my photograph of Orion's Belt in a competition. I didn't win but did get a constellation prize.

Graham Cann

HOLIDAYS

If I sprinkle myself in salt and pepper and then go abroad, does that make me a seasoned traveller?

There's a new travel guide highlighting towns and cities with badly laid paving slabs. It's called Trip Advisor.

I was staying in a hotel last night. I phoned down to reception and asked for a wake-up call. She said 'You're in your mid 40's, living with your mother and have achieved nothing in life'.

I told my suitcases there will be no vacation this year. Now I'm dealing with emotional baggage.

I was thinking about going on a cruise around Norway but I just couldn't afjord it.

I couldn't afford Tenerife this year. Is there a Fiverife?

Went to Scotland for my holidays five years running. Next time I'm taking a train.

So I went to the travel agents and said to the lady 'How do I get to a country near Sweden? She said 'Norway?' I said 'There must be...'

I got on a plane and was surrounded by boxes, jiffy bags and envelopes. Turned out it was a package holiday.

HUMAN BODY

I lost my hair years ago but I still carry a comb. I just can't part with it.

I was so close to winning the World's Most Congested Nose competition. But, at the last minute, I blew it.

I really do have a flat stomach – it's just that the L is silent.

If I had to get rid of one part of my body it would be my spine. Sometimes I think it's holding me back.

Eyelashes are supposed to prevent things from getting into your eyes but when I do have something in my eye it's always an eyelash. How eyeronic!

The skeleton didn't want to go to school because his heart wasn't in it.

I've just had a tattoo of Italy done on my chest. Now I've got sore Naples.

<u>JOBS</u>

Someone just rang me, sneezed, blew their nose and then hung up. I hate cold callers.

I've been a bit skint on the run up to Halloween so I've taken another job with my mate – we've been making plastic Draculas. I'm literally making every second Count.

I used to work at Kwik Fit. I left because I was always tyred and exhausted.

Does a railway worker have to be trained?

My boss told me that if I can get through today without mentioning biscuits he'll give me £100. Nice......

I got sacked today for watching porn on the works computer and making everything crash. My mate said he thought that was a bit harsh for watching porn. I said 'They don't mess about at flight control.'

I'm struggling with my chiropody business.....I'm still finding my feet.

My uncle was fired from a clock maker's factory yesterday. Apparently he sat there making faces all day.

I build bungalows. I used to build houses but that's another storey.

I'm starting up a company in Wales making push switches. The factory's in Prestatyn.

I've just handed in my notice as a drill operator on an offshore oil rig. It was so boring.

I always ring in sick on Mondays. My doctor has diagnosed me with a weekend immune system.

Before I became a stuntman, I trained to make mattresses just in case I needed something to fall back on.

Do people who work in a matches factory ever strike?

In a previous job, my boss said 'You're the worst train driver I've ever seen. How many trains have you derailed in the last year?' I said 'I'm not sure, it's hard to keep track'.

Just been for an interview for a job as a lathe operator. They turned me down.

I've packed in my job at Subway. They can get someone else to fill that role.

I've started making boats in my garage and I've got to say that sails are going through the roof.

My friend was fired from his lumberjack job after failing to cut down a tree eight times. He had exceeded the maximum number of loggin' attempts.

I went for a job interview and the guy told me to fill in the questionnaire so I went back down to the front door and beat up the doorman.

I went for a job interview on a building site mixing sand, cement and aggregates. I think I got the job but nothing's concrete yet.

My friend is returning to his job at the sewage works after an illness. He's missed his mates and said he's looking forward to seeing all the old faeces again.

Whenever I had to stand up and speak in class at my Junior School, I'd pee my pants. Almost ruined my teaching career.

The man who makes the giant eclairs at our local patisserie is retiring next month. When he leaves, there'll be some big chouxs to fill.

I quit my job at the cat shelter. I had no choice as they reduced meowers.

I'm just home from my first day as a hairdresser. Tired? I'm completely lacquered.

Whenever I go the extra mile for my clients, they just get very angry. I sometimes wonder why I ever became a taxi driver.

I had to leave my job at the sewerage works. I was just going through the motions......

I once interviewed for a position to become a blacksmith. They asked if I'd ever shooed a horse. I said 'No, but I've told a donkey to piss off'.

My worst ever job? Putting soft drinks in order of fizziness. It was soda grading.

I recently got laid off from the sugar packing plant. I'm sad but they put a little extra in my last pay packet as a sweetener.

Great news! I just got a job making chess games. I start on knights.

I've recently found out that lining up staff and pushing them over is frowned upon at Domino's.

People become butchers because they like to meat people.

I used to build stairs for a living but it's a very up and down business.

I just got the job of Senior Director at Old McDonald's Farm. I'm the CIEIO.

If we're going to arm teachers, then at least give librarians silencers.

I'm looking forward to my forthcoming job in toilet paper production. It's a new roll for me.

Pathologist: Someone who studies kerbs and pavements.

A worker has fallen into a vat at the Branston factory. Management say he is in a right pickle.

I've just retired after fifty years as a tool maker. It was a bit of a wrench.

I've been trying to offer my bookkeeping services to food critics and wine professionals to develop a specialist practice but so far no joy. It seems there's no accounting for taste.

Despite A level results of A,B,B,A, I can't find an employer to take a chance on me.

Since I lost my job at the adhesives factory, I've completely fallen to pieces.

It's really annoying the way people come round when I'm trying to work. To be honest, it's ruined my career as an anaesthetist.

LAW AND ORDER

Breaking News: A man arrested for stealing fireworks has been let off.

Today I saw a very short prisoner climbing down a wall. As he turned and sneered at me, I thought 'That's a little condescending'.

Police say a third of crime goes unreported. How do they know?

I got a rollicking off a policeman yesterday. He said I was loitering. I said a man told me to watch that dog shit and he hasn't come back yet.

Police have found a getaway car with an incomplete set of stolen golf clubs. They're still looking for the driver.

What do you call the security outside a Samsung store? Guardians of the Galaxy.

Polce toay announce they are nvestgatng a strng of ID thefts.

I've been shoplifting baby biscuits all day. I think life is all about taking rusks.

Somebody keeps sending me flowers with their heads cut off. I think I'm being stalked.

The detective entered the room. The blinds were drawn. But the furniture was real.

Police have stated that they believe Sooty and Sweep are the masterminds behind a recent crime wave. They also strongly believe someone else may have had a hand in it.

'Bill Stickers Will Be Prosecuted'. Sixty plus years since I first read that sign. Did they ever get him?

When the police arrested me for illegally downloading the entire Wikipedia, I said 'Wait! I can explain everything'.

I asked the Chief Inspector 'What are those pictures on your wall?' He said 'They're pictures of wanted criminals'. I said 'Why the hell didn't you arrest them when you took their photos?'

A police officer turned up at my door this morning.
'Do the letters TG mean anything to you?'
'No' I said.
'What about PR?'
'No, means nothing to me'.
'How about AH?'
'Look' I said. 'Am I suspected of something?'
'No, sir' he replied. 'These are just initial enquiries'.

Policeman: 'Name please?'
Man: 'Wizard of Oz'.
Policeman: 'Your *full* name, sir'.
Man: 'Wizard of Ounces'.

I once made a gun out of potatoes. It was a weapon of mash destruction.

A man was mugged yesterday by two men who hit him over the head with a bag of potatoes. The police asked him if he'd recognise them again and he said 'Yes, they were King Edwards'.

I told my girlfriend I was a barrister. She went mad when she walked into Costa and saw me making a cappuccino.

A lorry load of oranges has been stolen. Police are a peeling for information.

My friend's in prison for flashing. He can't bare it anymore.

The seminar 'How to Avoid Scams' has been cancelled. Tickets are non-refundable.

Someone broke into my home and stole my external hard drive. They really got my back-up.

Lots of violence could have been prevented in the old West if only cowboy architects had made the towns big enough for everyone.

I saw two men mugging an old lady and I asked myself if I should help but decided that three would be overkill.

A police officer started crying today as he was writing me a speeding ticket. I said 'Why are you crying?' He said 'It was a moving violation'.

Bloody thieves have stolen our newly planted tree. I say bring back the birch.

There's a man going round town throwing boxes of Corn Flakes and Rice Krispies at the windows of houses. Police describe him as a cereal offender.

A consignment of apples has been stolen from a lorry on the M1. Police are asking anyone with in-cider information to come forward.

A policeman stopped me last night. He said 'Get out of your car and walk towards me'. I did that. He said 'You're staggering'. I said 'You're not too bad yourself'.

The defence was tense, the accused bemused, the jury in a fury but the judge didn't budge. It was poetic justice.

What does a plain clothes policeman wear when off duty?

I stopped at the side of the road and dumped 10,000 bluebottles out of my van. I was done for fly tipping.

Police say they are baffled as to why a commemorative plaque outside the Colgate head office keeps being removed.

I was the getaway driver for a robbery at a paper factory in Bristol last night. We took the A4.

There's no better feeling than laying next to the person you love and they don't know you love them or that you're in their house again.

Graham Cann

MEN

I think I've just seen Quasimodo. If it wasn't him it was a dead ringer.

I saw what looked like a gravestone at the side of the road. It was for the oldest man in the world. Miles from London. He was 201.

The best men are like coffee. They're rich, hot and can keep you up all night.

Why are men like lino? If you're able to lay them correctly the first time, then you can walk all over them for the next twenty five years.

Why is it so hard for women to blink during foreplay? There just isn't enough time.

What is the useless bit of skin at the end of a penis? A man.

What do you call a man buried for 2000 years? Pete.

If you believe that the quickest way to a man's heart is his stomach, you know that you are aiming a little too high.

I sent my man a 'Get Better Soon' card. He's not sick, I just think he could do better.

I'm so tired of jokes about gays. I mean, come on guys.

Someone told me today that I didn't know how to shave correctly. Bloody cheek!

Men at 26 play football, men at 40 play tennis, men at 60 play golf. Have you noticed every time you get older, your balls get smaller?

Sad news for the guy with wooden legs whose house caught fire. The house was saved but he was burnt to the ground.

I know a bloke with one leg called Dave. I'm not sure what the other leg's called.

A friend told me that he used milk instead of shaving foam. 'Pasteurised?' 'No, just around my chin'.

Graham Cann

MIXED BAG

You can't get 12" rulers any longer.

I was going to tell a joke about punching something but then I realised it would be near the knuckle.

Gravity is important but if you remove it, you get gravy.

I saw a man going up a hill with a trolley full of four-leaf clovers, horseshoes and rabbits' feet. I thought 'He's pushing his luck.'

I keep thinking I'm holding an invisible pack of playing cards. No-one knows what I'm dealing with.

I dreamt I was eating my quilt. I woke up feeling a little down in the mouth.

I bought 25 bottles of Tippex today. Big mistake!

What's a foot long, made of leather and sounds like a sneeze? A shoe.

I went to a fancy dress party as a spider last night. God knows what time I crawled in.

For sale: Thick layer of dust. As seen on TV.

I tried doing a stand-up show online last night on Zoom but no-one thought I was funny. Not even remotely....

If you go to Greenwich and everything's closed, what do you do in the mean time?

I bought one of those anti-bullying wrist bands. I say bought – actually I stole it off a short, fat, ginger kid.

You won't find me sitting on top of a bonfire on 5th November. I'm just not that type of guy.

I've just passed my Communism exam. I got full Marx.

A pun is not completely matured until it is full groan.

Anyone ever tried eating a clock? It's very time consuming especially if you go back for seconds.

Five out of three people have trouble understanding fractions.

To whoever stole my Microsoft Office, I will find you. You have my Word.

Last night in my sleep I was thinking of the number 0.999999. Turns out it was a recurring dream.

Sometimes I put my head between my legs and lean forward. That's just how I roll.....

'What do we want?'
'HEARING AIDS!'
'When do we want them?'
'HEARING AIDS!'

I was very lonely so I bought some shares. It's nice to have a bit of company.

I've never worn my gay sweater. It hasn't come out of the closet yet.

6:30 has got to be the best time - hands down.

My ceiling isn't the best but it's up there.

Client: 'How much to answer three questions?'
Lawyer: '£500'.
Client: That's expensive, isn't it?'
Lawyer: 'Yes, now what's your third question?'

Where do bad rainbows go? Prism.

What's the difference between light and hard? You can fall asleep with the light on.

I found a rock yesterday which actually measured 1760 yards in length. Must be something of a milestone.

A big shout out to the people asking what the opposite of 'in' is.

Just saw a thickset man carrying loads of weapons and he even had one hanging out of his backside. It was a big arse 'n' all.

A priest, a minister and a rabbit walk into a blood bank. The rabbit says 'I think I might be a type O'.

Bullets are weird. They only do their job *after* they're fired.

A storm blew away 25% of my roof last night. Oof!

While most puns make me feel numb, mathematical puns make me feel number.

Exaggerations went up by two trillion percent last year.

I called the Child Abuse Hotline. A kid answered, called me a fat bastard and then told me to piss off.

My least favourite colour is purple. I hate it more than red and blue combined.

Then there's the mathematician who's afraid of negative numbers. He'll stop at nothing to avoid them.

We tried Plan a b, c, and d but none have worked. But Plan e might take off and Plan t is also growing on me.

Are blazers just smoking jackets that got out of control?

If the temperature is zero outside today and it's going to be twice as cold tomorrow, how cold will it be?

If you hold a coconut shell to your ear, you'll hear the sound of a one-legged horse standing still.

What do you call a piece of wood that has nothing to do? Board.

I wanted to come up with a joke about a cash machine but I can't think of one ATM.

Yes. Is time travel possible?

Apparently eight out of ten people don't believe in statistics.

Can anyone give me a rough idea how much a ballpark would cost?

I dreamt I was attacked by 500 sheets of paper. Phew!! It was just a bad ream.

I ate ten batteries yesterday. I think I excelled myself.

What did they call a photographic memory before the 1850's?

I know this may make me sound big-headed but I can't get my jumper off.

We've just had a massive amount of bubble wrap delivered to us by mistake. I said to my wife 'What shall we do with it?' She said 'Pop it in the shed'.

Russian roulette. You win some, you lose one.

Just saw two door bells having a fight. It was a right old ding dong.

Graham Cann

MUSIC

I just got hit with a rhythm stick. Am I entitled to an Ianjury claim?

I thought I could hear Bee Gee songs coming from my herb garden. It turned out to be Chive Talking.

If you say 'Space Ghettos' out loud in an American accent, it sounds like Spice Girls in a Scottish accent.

Does anyone know what the knights in white sat in?

During that whole journey through the desert, surely he could have thought of a name for the horse.

What's the first sign of Madness? Suggs walking up your driveway.

Alison Moyet's ex was caught stealing from the baker's. He took a whole lot of muffin for a handful of nothing.

I've just bought an ABBA toilet. What a loo!

I fell asleep, face down in a curry listening to REM. That's me in the korma......

My friend composes songs about sewing machines. He's a Singer songwriter.

My mate failed his Aboriginal music exam so I asked him 'Did you redo it?'

Just had to help Cat Stevens fix his caravan. Awning had broken.

A musician got arrested for stealing another guy's mandolin. Serves him right for luting.

My favourite sole singers are Pike and Tina Tuna.

For my next trick, I'll eat a percussion instrument in a bap. Drum roll please.

A coach load of musicians has broken down on the M5 blocking two lanes. Police have warned of some lengthy jams.

Accordion to a recent survey, replacing words with the names of musical instruments in a sentence often goes undetected.

My group, 'The Cat's Eyes', do mostly middle of the road stuff. My last band, 'The Duvets' did covers.

I got chucked out of the disco last night. All I did was request the DJ play my favourite Coldplay song. They said I was asking for Trouble.

The Devon and Cornwall Rock Festival has been cancelled because organisers couldn't agree whether the Jam or Cream should go on first.

I'm playing Scrabble with Midge Ure. I've got four letter left but they mean nothing to me – OVNR.

What is Mozart doing right now? Decomposing.

I stayed the night at the YMCA. I don't want to make a song and dance of it.

I didn't attend church today and listened to REM instead. Guess I'm losing my religion.

Listening to some old 70's pop tunes last night made me wince. 'I've Got You' by The Dooleys was one in particular.

My wife said she's leaving me if I don't get treatment for my obsession with Neil Diamond. 'I am' I said.

I once went to an Earth, Wind and Fire concert and was actually invited backstage and met Earth and Fire. I passed Wind in the corridor.

Rick Astley has admitted he's not very good at custard pie fights. He said 'I'd never run around and dessert you'.

I'm currently being hounded online by a guy called Buster who is constantly sending me recordings of 70's pop songs. Does anyone know the way, there's got to be a way, to block Buster.

I've just read that Hawaii have decided to hold a festival dedicated to a Glaswegian singer from the 60's. They're going to honour Lulu.

I'm currently birdwatching with Sinead O'Connor. So far, it's been seven owls and fifteen jays....

Why is my guitar making a screeching noise whenever I turn up the volume? Feedback would be appreciated.

If Benny and Bjorn of Abba were called Steve and Dan, they would have been known as ASDA.

Apparently Neil Diamond's real name is Neil Carbon. His record company put him under extreme pressure to change it.

If you stuff a gherkin inside a flute, you'll get a piccolo.

Sad to hear Elton John's coloured African frog has died. Goodbye yellow sick toad.

I've just witnessed the sad sight of my brother smashing up all his old Motown records. It was soul destroying.

Graham Cann

NATURE

There's something shady about trees.

I bought a bottle of head lice treatment yesterday but there are no instructions on how to use it. To be perfectly honest it's left me scratching my head.

When I was out walking the other day I saw a tree covered in bacon and when I went to take a closer look, I got mugged. Turned out it was a hambush.

I can cut down a tree using only my vision. It's true! I saw it with my own eyes.

If you're having a blind date on a glacier, don't break the ice.

Time for the Bird of Prey quiz. Fingers on buzzards.......

If you thought the most common owl was a Tawny, you'd be wrong. It's the Teet Owl.

NEIGHBOURS

The bloke next door's called Al Gebra. I could never work him out.

My neighbour has recently been coming into our garden and stealing beetroots. This morning I caught him red handed.

My neighbour passed away last night from severe indigestion. Can't believe Gav is gone.

As I was getting into bed she said 'You're drunk!' I said 'How do you know?' She said 'Because you live next door'.

My neighbour gave birth to piglets last night. Her husband's looking for the swine who did it.

My next door neighbour does a lot of hoarding. He's a junkie.

With no job and no money to buy food, I went begging to a neighbour. He was struggling too and could only lend me some herbs. So now I'm living on borrowed thyme.

PEOPLE

If you don't know what makes a human cloning machine, that makes two of us.

Sadly, the most prolific user of Facebook has died. We'll never see his like again.

I was walking down the street and I slipped on some dog poo. As I was getting up, a man came along and did the same. As he got up I said 'I just did that'. He then punched me in the face.

How do so many people get simple sayings wrong? Answers on a coastguard please.

Is it just me or are circles pointless?

People are shocked when they find out I'm not good with electrics.

I asked my barber what kind of cut would make me look good. A power cut wasn't the reply I was looking for.

It annoys me when people use incorrect punctuation?

I think that people who shorten their name to Pat are missing a trick.

I gave the postman a right shock this morning by going to the door naked. I'm not sure which scared him most...my naked body or the fact I knew where he lived.

I've only ever seen people overwhelmed or underwhelmed but never whelmed properly.

People who don't finish their sentences

What's the difference between Iron Man and Iron Woman? One is a superhero, the other is a simple instruction.

I hate it when people use metaphors that are physically impossible. It makes my blood boil.

I fell in love with a mountaineer's daughter. She wasn't much to look at but she had a lovely Pyrenees.

I went to my barber's and told him to give me a pony tail. He said 'Once upon a time, this pony went to the seaside….'

I grew up in a really tough area. Gangs roaming the streets and putting cream on your head and topping it off with a cherry. Yeah, life was tough in the gateau.

Why do people use quotes and catchphrases incorrectly? Still, no use crying over spilt salt.

A feller in the bar asked me what it's like to be married. I said 'Amaze'. He said 'Don't you mean amazing?' I said 'No, I mean it's hard to get out of.'

Some people say 'If you can't beat them, join them'. I say 'If you can't beat them, beat them' because they will be expecting you to join them, so you will have the element of surprise.

Do you know what makes me cross? The lollipop lady.

Her body tensed and quivered as wave after wave surged through it. I probably should've told her about the electric fence.

You'd have to stoop pretty low to pickpocket a midget.

It takes pirates so long to learn the alphabet because they can spend years at C.

've got one word to say to my amazing former maths teacher. Thank you.

ust trying to gauge people's opinion – How much do you hink I should spend on a bottle of wine? Is 15 minutes too ong?

Three men on a boat. They have four cigarettes but 1othing to light them with. So they throw one cigarette overboard and the whole boat becomes a cigarette lighter.

Why did the blind man fall down the well? He didn't see hat well.

People are making apocalypse jokes like there's no comorrow.

met a transvestite from the Greater Manchester area in che pub last night. He had a Wigan address.

I'm done with being a people pleaser.   As long as everyone's OK with that…….

Three conspiracy theorists walk into a bar. You can't tell me that's just a coincidence.

People often ask if my French jokes are immature….wee.

I'm never smoking weed with immigrants again. I asked 'Anyone have any papers?' and they all legged it.

I was admiring a farmer's field yesterday. The farmer said it was arable but I rather liked it.

There was this midget called Pete who was telling me that currently he's a baker who specialises in flatbreads. I love the pitta patter of tiny Pete.

According to a new report out today, about half the world's population is overweight. That's a little under 4 billion people. These are just round figures of course.

People scoff at the way I eat cake.....which I find ironic.

A bloke on a tractor has just driven past me shouting 'The end of the world is nigh'. It was Farmer Geddon.

To be frank, I'd have to change my name.

My window cleaner just went absolutely berserk banging on my door shouting and swearing. I think he's lost his rag.

I remember the time when you could practise dunking ginger nuts. These days they call that bullying.

Graham Cann

PETS

My cat swallowed a ball of wool a few months ago. She's just had mittens.

My cat went missing yesterday. I walked around the local area for half an hour but no luck. My wife said I needed to look harder. So I shaved my head and got some tattoos on my knuckles but I still couldn't find him.

If you've got a dog called Shark, never take him to the beach.

If I have to have my cat put down, do I need to book nine appointments at the vets?

I spotted a pure white Dalmatian yesterday. It was the least I could do.

My dog chases everybody on a bike. So I locked his bike up.

Think twice before getting a rescue cat. My nan got one. She tripped and fell one day and it just sat there and did nothing.

I've put my dog on a vegan diet. He's eaten three so far.....

I bought a dog from a blacksmith. When I got him home he made a bolt for the door.

Crufts have gone bust. They've called in the retrievers.

I just told my wife I'd been bitten by an Alsatian on my walk. She said 'My God, what if it had been a small child?' I said 'I could have fought off a small child!'

You know it's cold outside when you trip over dog shite instead of standing in it.

As a child I owned a cat which had this rather odd fascination with Japanese electronics. Today, on the anniversary of her passing, I'd like to propose a toast......To Sheba.

I've named my dog Five Miles. It's just so I can say I walk five miles every day.

I've finally bought my wife a pug for her birthday. Sticky-out eyeballs, flat nose and wrinkly skin – still, the dog seems to like her.

I can't take my dog to the pond anymore because the ducks keep attacking him. Guess that's what I get for having a pure bread dog.

I went to the pet shop and asked for 12 bees. The assistant counted out 13 bees and handed them over. I said 'You've given me one too many'. He said 'That one's a freebie'.

Do dogs ignore calls to their mobiles if there's no collar ID?

Cats are useless at storytelling because they only have one tale.

I've got a cat called Potato. Must remember to get him chipped.

My dog only responds to commands in Spanish. He's Espanyol.

I insured my car yesterday. When I finished the man said 'Do you have any pets?' I said 'I have a dog'. He said 'Would you like me to insure him also?' I said 'No thanks. He doesn't drive'.

My pet pig has lost its voice. It's feeling very disgruntled.

Graham Cann

POLITICS

Later today, The Prime Minister will be holding a meeting with the Cabinet. Tomorrow, he'll be talking to the dressing table and dining room chair.

What's the difference between a politician and a flying pig? The letter F.

I wasn't allowed in the House of Commons because I was circumcised. Apparently, you need to be a complete dick.

RELIGION

threw a bottle of Domestos at our vicar yesterday. I was charged with bleach of the priest.

got sacked as a tour guide of the Vatican City. As I was talking about the Pope, we turned a corner and I said 'Ah, speak of the devil.'

ehovah's Witnesses don't celebrate Halloween. I guess they don't like random people knocking on their doors.

Fortunately, the streaker who ran naked through the church was apprehended by the priest and grabbed by the organ.

When I visited a monastery last week, one of the monks was chopping potatoes. I said 'Are you the chip monk?' He said 'No, I'm the deep fat friar'.

If Christ were alive today, he'd have a huge retirement account ....because Jesus saves.

The first tennis match recorded in the Bible was wher Joseph served in Pharaoh's court.

I've heard Jesus drives a Christler.

My girlfriend just admitted she used to be a Christian so broke up with her. It might seem judgmental but I have only known her since she was Christine.

What do you call a sleepwalking nun? A roamin' Catholic.

My vicar went missing yesterday. I had to fill out a missing parsons report.

If you get an email with the subject 'Knock,knock' don't open it! It's a Jehovah's Witness working from home.

I got stuck behind Satan in the queue at the Post Office. The devil takes many forms.

Graham Cann

SCIENCE AND TECHNOLOGY

I hear that the demand for helium is on the rise.

Scientists have found that trees can communicate with one another. They use 'What's Sap'.

I've just bought myself the George Formby Antivirus for my computer. It's very good at cleaning Windows.

What did our parents do to kill boredom before the internet? My 26 brothers and sisters don't know either.

Does anybody know how long it takes to repair a hearing aid? I posted it two weeks ago and I've heard nothing since.

It was a sad and disappointing day when I discovered my Universal Remote Control did not, in fact, control the Universe.

Einstein wrote a scientific paper about space. It's about time too!

I've just bought a wooden computer but I'm having difficulty logging on.

Can anyone tell me how we can land a spacecraft on a comet travelling at 2000mph but we can't make a car park machine that gives out change?

A robot's favourite Mexican dish is a Silicon Carne.

You can't use 'beefstew' as a password. It's not stroganoff.

If you get an email message about canned meat, whatever you do, do not open it! It's spam.

Why doesn't the Sun go to college? Because it has a million degrees.

I changed my password to 'incorrect' so whenever I forget what it is, the computer will say 'Your password is incorrect'.

Protons have mass. I didn't even know they were Catholic.

The computer hackers got away from the scene of the crime. They ransomeware.

My IT friend tried to flirt with a waitress and failed miserably. I guess it wasn't the first time he couldn't connect to the server.

I'm a research scientist who's analysing bestiality between humans and dogs. If you'd like more details, I'll be in my Lab.

Hackers brought down my online business but I managed to keep the website address – that's domain thing.

I just can't get away from my broken keyboard. There's no Escape.

My friend claims that he can print a gun using his 3D printer but I'm not impressed. I've had a Canon printer for years.

NASA are sending traditionalist Christians to the red planet. Amish on to Mars.

Any astronaut dying in space has an orbituary written for them.

Set your wifi password to 24446666668888888. So when someone asks for it, tell them it's 12345678.

Good news! Scientists have successfully grown human vocal chords in a petri dish. The results speak for themselves.

Graham Cann

SELF ANALYSIS

I tried taking a selfie in the shower but it keeps coming out blurry. I have selfie steam issues.

If I had to describe myself in three words, I would say 'Not very good at maths'.

Graham Cann

SEX

Why can't men find the G spot? Because they refuse to ask for directions.

I've just slept with a girl who said I was the only one she's ever slept with. I was feeling good until she said she gave all the others 8, 9 or 10 out of 10.

I thought I was great in bed until I found out my girlfriend has asthma.

I am a sex object! Every time I ask a woman for sex, she objects.

I took this girl home last night and I said to her 'How do you like your eggs in the morning?' She said 'Unfertilised'.

It's customary to call a nun, after she's had a sex change operation, a transistor.

Of course I believe in safe sex. I've got a handrail round my bed.

Four words to destroy a man's ego – 'Is it in yet?'

Genders are like the Twin Towers. There used to be two and now it's a sensitive subject.

'Give it to me! Give it to me!' she yelled. 'I'm so wet, give it to me now!' She could scream all she wanted to. I was keeping the umbrella.

I asked a Chinese girl for her number. She said 'Sex! Sex! Sex! Free sex tonight!' I said 'Wow!' Then her friend said 'She means 666-3629'.

Why is sex like maths? You add a bed, subtract the clothes, divide the legs and pray there's no multiplying.

Why is prostitution illegal? Because when it comes to screwing people and taking their money, the government doesn't want anyone outperforming them.

Once, my parents walked in on me masturbating. Why they were walking around masturbating is beyond me.

I got excited when I had to attend a class for daily sex. Turns out it was for dyslexia.

I was asked if I believed in sex before marriage. I'm all for it as long as it doesn't prolong the ceremony.

I want to tell my girlfriend she's using way too much teeth when she goes down on me but I don't want to hurt her feelings. How do I soften the blow?

The life cycle of the male sex drive:
Age 16-32 : Tri-weekly
Age 32-55 : Try-weekly
Over 55 : Try-weakly

What has a singer and the coin return on a Durex machine got in common? Johnny Cash.

Surprise sex is the best thing to wake up to. Unless you're in prison.

SHOPPING

I couldn't stop buying perfume and aftershave. I had hundreds of bottles. People said I had more scents than money.

My friend has just opened a shop in the West Indes selling glass cooking pots. It's called Pyrex of the Caribbean.

The Liverpool branch of WH Smith's has taken down the sign saying 'Pocket Calculators' after finding that most customers thought it was an instruction.

I had to have a crap in the toilet but it wouldn't flush. I've now been banned from B&Q.

Asda have just announced that staff have been stealing Oxo cubes. This was discovered during stock taking.

I was in Asda and I asked an assistant what gets rid of germs. She said 'Ammonia cleaner'. I said 'Sorry, I thought you worked here'.

I saw someone stealing in the Apple store. I've been called as an iWitness.

The girl who operates the sunbeds in my local beauty salon is Tanya.

A stressed little old lady in Tescos asked me if I could see the least busy checkout for her. 'Far queue' I said. The feisty old girl hit me with her handbag and walked off.

I just phoned up for some incontinence pads. They asked where I was ringing from. I told them 'From the waist down'.

The sweater I bought recently kept picking up static electricity so I returned it to the store. They gave me another one, free of charge.

There's a new perfume on the market called Donkey. It's by Christian D'Eeyore.

I went to the butcher today and asked 'Do you have a sheep's head?' He replied 'No, it's just the way I part my hair'.

I bought a new pair of gloves yesterday but they're both lefts' which, on the one hand is great, but on the other, it's just not right.

I made a mistake at the grocery store. I went to get six Sprites but accidentally picked 7Up.

Announcement in Tesco – 'Checkout Supervisor on Till 3 Please'. I had a look and yes, she's rather nice.

A bloke walks into a stationer's: 'Have you got a Bulldog clip?' The assistant said 'No, but I've got a nice video of a Terrier'.

I've just ordered a chicken and an egg from Amazon.....I'll let you know.

IKEA have been taken to court over faulty luggage. I hear prosecutors are having a really difficult time putting a case together.

SPORT

Just hit a record 63 on my local golf course. Now on to the 2nd hole.

My wife left me today because she thinks I'm more interested in football than her. We were married for 6 seasons.

What do you call a nervous javelin thrower? Shakespeare.

I had to pull out of the World Championship for fire eaters. I wasn't match fit.

I was in a horse race nearing the finish line when I got hit in the eye with an apple seed. I was pipped at the post.

My wife's left me. She said I watch too much cricket. It's really hit me for 6.

I went swimming at our local baths yesterday and had a wee in the deep end. The lifeguard blew his whistle so loud I nearly fell in.

I joined the cricket team but I'm having trouble rubbing my legs together as loud as the others.

There was this bloke in the pub last night boasting that he used to play rugby for Wasps. Myself, I'd have preferred cash.

My golf coach has identified that I'm standing too close to the ball......after I've hit it.

I've invented a new sport called silent tennis. It's like normal tennis but without the racket.

The world's worst boxer has finally put his life story on YouTube. He's had over one million hits.

Quasimodo was walking down the street with twenty kids chasing him. He turned round and said 'F off! I ain't got ya football'.

Just finished reading 'Improve Your Golf' by A T Knowles.

IKEA's football team is playing tonight. Their manager Alan Key is expected to line up with a flatpack four.

Chris Ewbank is a religious guy. He punches people in the faith.

After winning the game, I decided to throw the ball to the spectators. Apparently, that's frowned upon in bowling.

My friend Ty came first in the Beijing marathon at the Olympics but still hasn't been awarded a gold medal. China refuses to acknowledge Ty won.

At the Olympics I saw a man carrying a long stick and I asked 'Are you a pole vaulter?' He said 'No. I am German but how did you know my name was Walter?'

It was so hot in the stadium after the baseball game because all the fans left.

My dog Minton ate all my shuttlecocks. Bad Minton.

Fish have never been good tennis players. They don't like getting close to the net.

I was at the climbing centre the other day but someone had stolen all the grips from the wall. Honestly, you couldn't make it up.

What's a horse's favourite sport? Stable tennis.

My boxing trainer said we should have a spar. So I put on my gloves and headgear. I'm the first to admit that I was a little overdressed for a manicure.

A jockey was fined last week for racist behaviour.

Did you know Paul Gascoigne donated one of his England jerseys to Yasser Arafat's family? The old boy asked to be buried in Gazza Strip.

My brother goes running in the Derbyshire Dales. It keeps him in Peak fitness.

The local ballet took part in a charity football match. It ended up 2-2.

SUPERNATURAL

Why do spiritualists and mediums have doorbells?

A ghost floated into a pub and asked for a pint of bitter. 'Sorry' said the barman 'We don't serve spirits here'.

What do ghosts serve for dessert? I scream.

I have this weird talent where I can identify what's inside a wrapped present. It's a gift.

I once told a bad joke about ghosts. It still haunts me to this day.

Not to brag, but I have sychic powers. For example, right now you're thinking 'It's psychic, idiot!'

Here's a question for all you mind readers out there....

What do they use at Hogwarts to read PDF's? A dobby.

I remember thinking as I sellotaped a Ouija board to a boomerang, 'This is going to come back to haunt me'.

TRANSPORT

A lorry carrying Vic's Vapour Rub crashed on the M6. Luckily no congestion for 8 hours.

I picked up a hitch hiker yesterday and after a while he asked me if I was scared that he was a serial killer. I said 'What are the chances of two in one car?'

While on the underground I taught my dog to play the trumpet. Barking to Tooting in 15 minutes.

A lorry carrying snooker accessories overturned on the M1 yesterday. There were cues for miles.

A man hit by a rental car says 'It Hertz.'

I've just spend £300 on a limousine and discovered that the fee doesn't include a driver. I can't believe I've spent all that money and nothing to chauffeur it.

After being escorted out of King's Cross station with concussion, I'm beginning to think my Hogwart's acceptance letter was a hoax.

I've had four new tyres fitted to my Golf and now I've got a hole in one.

I spotted a beautiful sports car in town recently. After chatting to the owner, he lifted the bonnet. I asked him why there were minestrone, tomato and mushroom marks all over the engine. He said it had been souped up.

I found a plane on our roof this morning. The wife had left the landing light on again.

took a car for a test drive with a salesman today. He asked me what my impression was of the car. I said 'Brum..brum...brummmmmmmm'.

've just bought a new satnav and it's incredible. Yesterday drove past a zoo and it said 'Bear left'.

My car manual says 'depress clutch to start'. I told it all my problems, but it still won't start.

What do you call a guy who used to like tractors? An extractor fan.

The taxi driver refused my tip last week. Fare enough.

Just had my car waxed. I never realised it was so hairy.

With the new electric Vauxhall Corsa, they're offering a test drive with no charge – seems a bit pointless.

What do you get if you cross the Atlantic with the Titanic? About half way.

What did the farmer say when he lost his tractor? 'Where's my tractor?'

I told my mate I was selling my car. He said 'How much?' I said 'All of it'.

Sometimes when I'm cruising around the city in a £300,000 vehicle, I often think 'If this bus driver doesn't speed up, I'm going to be late for work'.

I was surprised they wouldn't accept my Oyster card at the local Shell station.

I desperately needed to have a shite on the train today but there were no toilets in sight so I just sat there and held it for 20 minutes. The woman sitting opposite, looking at me in disgust, eventually said 'How long are you going to sit there with that poo in your hand?'

Did you know that if you took all the cars in the world and put them end to end, a BMW driver would pull out and try and pass them all?

While out driving my car today, I was rear-ended by an ice cream van. I'm now suffering with Mr Whippylash.

My car failed its emissions test today. Fuming!

Remember when air was free at a petrol station but now it's 50p. That's inflation for you.

I spotted something shiny in the road. It was a fork.

Roundabouts are never straight forward.

Graham Cann

WEDDINGS

I had a horsedrawn wedding. Big mistake. I should have hired a photographer.

It's common knowledge that the best man speech should only last as long as the groom can in bed.....and with that, I bid you good evening.

I married Miss Right. I just didn't know her first name was Always.

Marriage is like a deck of cards. In the beginning all you need is two hearts and a diamond. In the end, you wish you had a club and a spade.

My dad proposed to my mum at 11:59 on New Years Eve. He told me it was because he wanted to say she took all year to decide.

Mr Ohm remembered fondly the time he proposed to Mrs Ohm. He couldn't resistor.

I went to a wedding where all the guests ended up getting food poisoning from the buffet. It was a real party pooper.

Two florists got married. It was an arranged marriage.

Some mornings I wake up grumpy. And others, I just let him sleep in.

The most enjoyable part of a cannibal wedding is toasting the bride and groom.

WISE SAYINGS

Confucius says 'Man who runs behind a car will get exhausted but man who runs in front of car will get tired'.

Give a man a gun and he will rob a bank. Give a man a bank and he will rob everyone.

Accept that some days you are the pigeon and some days you are the statue.

Honesty is the best policy but insanity is the best defence.

Confucius says 'Man with no garden looks forlorn'.

Graham Cann

WOMEN

Two little boys were at a wedding when one leaned over to the other and asked 'How many wives can a man have?' 'Sixteen' was the reply. 'Four better, four worse, four richer, four poorer'.

I used to date a girl whose left eye was missing. He was a right looker.

Last night I had beef stew with dumplings. I really shouldn't call her that……

Women are being grossly overcharged for their Botox injections but when they see the bill, none of them look surprised.

I asked 50 women which conditioner they preferred in their shower. They said 'Who the hell are you and how did you get into my shower?'

Probably the worst thing you can hear when you're wearing your bikini is 'Good for you!'

Do you ever get one of those days when you wish Jolene would actually just take your man?

To the women who say 'Men are only interested in one thing'. Have you ever considered being more interesting?

If a woman sleeps with ten men, she's a slut. But if a man does it..........he's definitely gay.

WORDS

I hate people who use the same word twice in a sentence. Enough is enough!

How do you spell 'Caution Hot Surface' in Braille?

A crèche. A car accident involving posh people.

The first rule of the Thesaurus Club. Don't talk about, mention, speak of, converse, babble, discuss or gossip about the Thesaurus Club.

I can't believe the word 'gullible' looks like a cat when viewed upside down.

A truck loaded with thousands of copies of Roget's Thesaurus crashed yesterday losing its entire load.

Witnesses were stunned, startled, aghast, taken aback, dumbfounded, speechless......

I've taken a vowel of silnce.

I got a letter today from the Scrabble Society.

So I said to the decorator 'What is Satin Finish?' He said 'No idea but if it's any help I know what Chair is in Swedish'.

I was asked to give a word with no vowels but I couldn't think of one. In fact I think it's a myth that such words exist.

I'm not a snob but I confess that I find the overuse of foreign phrases in English conversation to be rather passé and somewhat fin de siècle.

own the world's worst thesaurus. Not only is it awful but t's awful.

was so bored that I memorised six pages of a dictionary. learnt next to nothing.

bought a dictionary and when I got it home I realised all the pages were blank. I have no words to describe how angry I am.

Aibohphobia is an irrational fear of palindromes.

hate it when people don't know the difference between your and you're. There so stupid.

'Can I have a quick word?' 'Velocity'.

Propaganda. A Yorkshireman just having a good look.

Most people write 'congrats' because they can't spell congratjulasyions.

Percussion. How upholsterers are paid.

WORLD

It's surprisingly cold in Argentina right now. It's bordering on Chile.

Just found out I've got a twin living in Australia. We were separated at Perth.

Is the leaning tower of Pisa a listed building?

I've just got back from China. I feel disorientated.

What do you call a Scotsman with diarrhoea? Bravefart.

There's been an outbreak of Bovine Norovirus in Austria. The hills are alive with the sound of moo sick.

There's a coin shortage in America. They're running out of common cents.

My Mexican uncle takes anti-anxiety medication. It's for Hispanic attacks.

India is a very peaceful country. Nobody has any beef over there.

Everyone knows where the Big Apple is but does anyone know where Minneapolis.

Does your sister like living in the wilderness north west of Canada? Dunno.......Alaska.

If you've ever seen Swedish warships with barcodes on them, it's because, when they dock, they can Scandanavian.

I asked a German if he knew what the square root of 81 was. He said 'No'.

What's the difference between an Aussie and a yogurt? A yogurt's got culture.

I called a suicide hotline in Afghanistan. They got all excited and asked if I could drive a truck.

Do they allow loud laughing in Hawaii or just a low ha?

My wife thinks I'm financially irresponsible. Wait till she finds out I've won the Nigerian lottery.

Why isn't Tripoli spelt eee?

I'm going to France tomorrow for the annual Flicking a Ruler on the Edge of a Desk competition. It's held annually in the Dordogne.

Graham Cann

AND FINALLY.....

I would like to sincerely thank all those readers who have made '1001 One-Liners and Short Jokes' series such a success and for posting so many positive reviews on Amazon. I appreciate you and am grateful to every one of you.

I hope you have found this collection entertaining and amusing and that you will spread the word by leaving a review on Amazon.

Hopefully with some positive reviews out there, others will grab a copy of the book and will be cheered up too. It's all about spreading a little laughter and joy.

Thank you so much!

CLAIM YOUR FREE GIVEAWAY HERE!

Don't forget your FREE book! All you have to do to receive this gag-tastic e-book is to use this link https://dl.bookfunnel.com/n90r726oa8 and I'll send you a copy free, gratis and on the house!

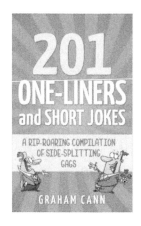

Not only will you receive a free joke book but I'll also enrol you as a member of **The 1001 One-Liners Club** where I send you a light-hearted email every Monday morning to get your week off to a flying start!

ABOUT THE AUTHOR

Graham Cann doesn't do drugs or drink. At his age, he gets the same effect just from standing up too fast. He remembers the Whirlybirds and Fireball XL5 for heaven sakes! Among his dare-devil activities are rambling, gardening and a smattering of DIY.

To be fair, he has taken the controls of a helicopter (but he did give them back!) and has sung on stage with Take That in front of 30,000 fans. He loves all things nostalgia, Zenning out and the odd one-liner joke or three.

Graham Cann

DO YOU LIKE READING?

WOULD YOU LIKE US TO SEND YOU FREE E-BOOKS?

That is what we do for every member of our Advance Readers Club.

We will send you a new Kindle book absolutely FREE prior to the publication date. All we ask is that you read it and then place an honest review on Amazon.

The range of books is non-fiction and we have sent out all types of e-books ranging from keto diets and puppy training manuals to mindfulness and joke books.

Just contact us now at info@chascannco.com and you will be added to a special list that we email every time a new book is released.

A selection of books from the same

publisher

For the full range, please go to

www.chascannco.com

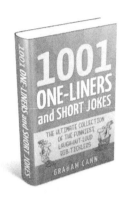

1001 One-Liners and Short Jokes

#1 Amazon Best Seller. They're all here in this **classic collection** of the **most hilarious one-liners** on planet Earth! This eye-watering compilation has been carefully selected to get your giggle glands going and is **guaranteed to give you hours of laughter and enjoyment.**

Each of the 1001 gags has been placed into its own category such as Addictions, Religion and Sex so **you can find a joke easily on any number of topics.** A wise sage once said, **"Laughter is, and will always be, the best form of therapy"** so go on, cheer yourself up with this **fabulous collection of mirth and merriment.**

1001 Dad Jokes

This is **the joke book no Dad should be without**! Crammed full of the **best Dad jokes ever** and filled with **fabulous funnies and humongous hilarities**!

- *What happened to the Pope when he went to Mount Olive? Popeye nearly killed him.*
- *Just got back from a day trip to The Helium Museum. I've got to say that I can't speak highly enough of the place.*
- *I had an ironic accident playing cricket. I got the runs.*

A real chuckle fest! Ideal for Father's Day, Birthdays, Christmas and special occasions.

Fantasy and Mystical Art Therapy Adult Colouring Book

Immerse yourself in an enchanting world of magical mystic while you take time out of your busy day.

• 50 **beautiful ethereal designs** catering for **all levels of artistic creativity**.

• **Intricate illustrations of beautiful women, fairies, unicorns, birds, nature, zen-tangle patterns** and so much more designed to exercise your imagination.

• Slow down and relax. **Feel that tension melt away** as you color and **rediscover your creativity**.

• **Ideal gift for Mothers' Day, Birthdays, Easter and Vacations.**

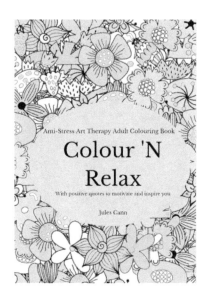

Colour 'n Relax Adult Colouring Book

◆ **150 pages of detailed, varied designs** catering for **all levels of artistic creativity,** including **uplifting quotes to inspire and motivate.**

◆ **Intricate illustrations of mandalas, flowers, swirling patterns** and so much more designed to **exercise your imagination.**

◆ **The ideal alternative to too much screen time.** Lose yourself as you focus your mind while you colour away your stress and anxiety.

◆ **Ideal gift for Mothers' Day, Birthdays, Easter and Vacations.**

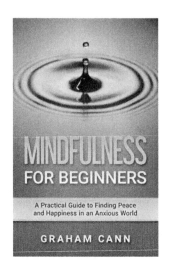

<u>Mindfulness for Beginners: A Practical Guide to Finding Peace and Happiness in an Anxious World</u>

Graham Cann brings a **wealth of experience** to the knowledge and practice of mindfulness and meditation gained over 50 years to produce an **excellent beginners' guide**. He will be sharing how, in just a few minutes each day, you can **relieve worry and stress** and emerge as **a new calmer, and more contented you!**

'Mindfulness for Beginners' is an **easy to read, step-by-step guide** that empowers you to take control of your mind and **bring peace to bear on your life** even in the most trying of circumstances.

Printed in Great Britain
by Amazon

14295876R00139